Original title: Difference or Love

Author: Kätriin Kaldaru
Editor: Jessica Elisabeth Luik
ISBN 978-9916-86-000-7

Difference or Love

Kätriin Kaldaru

Entangled Moments

In the web of time, we weave our tales,
Of fleeting glances and whispered gales,
Moments dance like fractured light,
Lost in shadows, cloaked in night.

Hearts enmeshed in silent cries,
Speaking truths beneath the skies,
Paths converge, then drift apart,
Echoes linger within the heart.

Threads that touch, then fade away,
Leaving dreams in soft decay,
A tapestry both fierce and frail,
In the web of time, we sail.

Forgotten Rhythms

Lost in beats of distant drums,
Where time has slipped and silence hums,
Echoes of a song long sung,
Whispered by the old and young.

A melody that once we knew,
Dances now in morning dew,
Chords that tug upon the mind,
Fading in the sands of time.

Forgotten rhythms pulse and sway,
Calling from another day,
In shadows deep, the notes resound,
Seeking where lost souls are found.

Bound by Minds

In a realm where thoughts align,
Hearts and souls in silent sign,
Words unspoken, yet so clear,
In the space where dreams appear.

Minds entangle, weave and blend,
In connections that transcend,
Bound by whispers, bound by light,
In the still and quiet night.

A dance of intellect and grace,
In this boundless, secret space,
Through the mind's immortal flight,
We are tethered in the night.

A Thousand Suns

In the blaze of dawning light,
A thousand suns ignite the night,
Each a beacon, burning bright,
Guiding through the endless fight.

Hope is kindled, fire anew,
In every heart, a sky of blue,
From the ashes, rise again,
Strength unyielding, free from pain.

Day and night, the cycle turns,
Through each star, a lesson learned,
In the blaze of dawning light,
A thousand suns ignite our might.

Soulful Threads

In the quiet hums of night,
Dreams are woven tight,
Stars whisper soft secrets,
In their beaming light.

Hearts beat in unseen patterns,
Threaded by love's embrace,
Woven letters of longing,
Time cannot erase.

Tales of ancient sorrows,
And of joyous mirth,
Spun into the tapestry,
Of our humble earth.

Each thread tells a story,
Of courage, love, and dread,
In the soulful quilt of life,
Upon which we tread.

Fragmented Moments

Shattered glass and broken time,
Moments lost in a rhyme,
Pieces of a forgotten day,
Scattered far away.

Whispers caught in the breeze,
Echoes of memories,
Fleeting glimpses of the past,
Fading shadows cast.

A laugh here, a tear there,
Fragments beyond repair,
In the puzzle of our lives,
More than mere archives.

Through the fragments, there we stand,
Holding hope in our hand,
Embracing the incomplete,
With hearts that understand.

Lost in Translation

Words float in the silence,
Meaning stirs beneath,
Silent voices speak out loud,
In the spaces between teeth.

Languages form barriers,
Thoughts are left unsaid,
Silent cries for connection,
Replace the words once read.

A bridge across the twilight,
Where meaning meets the soul,
Lost in translation's void,
We search to be whole.

In the whispers of our hearts,
True language is found,
Unspoken understanding,
In the love that surrounds.

Unspoken Truths

In the quiet of the night,
Where shadows intertwine,
Lie the unspoken truths,
That words cannot define.

Gestures reveal the whispers,
Hidden deep within,
Truths that linger softly,
Beneath our skin.

Eyes meet in silent speech,
Confessions in a glance,
Unveiling secret worlds,
In a fleeting chance.

Though lips may remain sealed,
Our hearts speak clear,
Unspoken truths shine bright,
When understanding is near.

Interwoven Essence

Threads of fate in twilight's veil,
Whisper secrets through the night.
In the tapestry of dreams,
Stars and hearts burn ever bright.

Woven tales of ancient lore,
Binding spirits, lost and found.
Echoes cross the time-worn shore,
In their song, we are bound.

Moonlit paths, where shadows blend,
Carry echoes from afar.
In the silence, spirits mend,
Guided by a distant star.

Interwoven, hearts and mind,
By a thread, we're all entwined.
In the dance of endless time,
Essence pure, undefined.

Stark Affinities

In a realm of stark reliefs,
Where emotions ebb and flow,
Two souls find affinity,
In the twilight's gentle glow.

Barren landscapes, hearts exposed,
Tender whispers soften stones.
In each gaze, a secret posed,
Love in stark affinities known.

Contrast paints a vivid scene,
Night and day, a perfect blend.
In the shadows, light is seen,
When the twilight finds its end.

Silent nights and quiet dreams,
Woven close by destiny.
In the heart's soft woven seams,
Stark affinities set free.

Beyond Boundaries

Past the edge where shadows fall,
Lies a world yet to explore.
Beyond boundaries, we stand tall,
Seeking whispers evermore.

Horizons blend in tender hues,
Limitations fade away.
Boundless dreams in nightly muse,
Guide us through the breaking day.

In the void where time expands,
Hope and fear are cast aside.
Hearts, unchained by cosmic hands,
Measure not where love abides.

Through the realms where spirits soar,
Boundless journeys do we take.
Beyond boundaries, we implore,
Magic realms for love's own sake.

Sundry Hearts

Among the realms of sundry hearts,
Differences do intertwine.
In the dance where love imparts,
Complex souls find light divine.

Woven dreams in myriad shades,
Rich diversity unfolds.
In the unity love wades,
Every heart a story holds.

Soft and gentle, fierce and wild,
Every beat a unique sound.
Through the laughter of a child,
Common threads of love are found.

Among the sundry hearts we find,
In the spectrum of the soul,
Light and dark, so interlined,
Making every spirit whole.

Veiled Warmth

Through gossamer threads of dawn's embrace,
Soft whispers of morning's kiss,
A gentle glow in a hidden place,
Where shadows form in timeless bliss.

The tender veil of a waking sun,
Holds secrets wrapped in gold,
Each moment born, a silken spun,
A story yet untold.

In the hush of early light,
Warmth hides behind the veil,
Promises whisper on the edge of night,
In dreams where hope prevails.

The world begins to stir and wake,
As soft warmth steals the show,
A tender kiss for morning's sake,
In veiled and gentle glow.

Through the shroud of waking day,
A soft warmth starts to rise,
In every ray and every stay,
The morning's sweet disguise.

Midnight Whispers

Beneath the cloak of midnight's gaze,
Stars whisper secrets old,
In silver threads and dreamy haze,
Their stories gently unfold.

The moonlight casts its quiet spell,
On waters dark and deep,
Midnight's whispers softly tell,
Of shadows that quietly creep.

Each whisper floats on velvet night,
A symphony so hushed,
In every breath, a hidden light,
Where darkness turns to blush.

The world in solemn silence sways,
To whispers of the hour,
As midnight lingers, softly prays,
In sweet and silent power.

In every corner, shadowed deep,
There lingers whispered tales,
The night holds secrets it won't keep,
In dark and quiet veils.

Fluid Contrasts

In the dance of light and shade,
Fluid contrasts form,
Through the ebb and flow displayed,
In patterns bold and warm.

The night and day, a braided weave,
Each moment they entwine,
A dance where opposites believe,
In harmony so fine.

Shadows merge with beams so bright,
In a ballet of hues,
Fluid contrasts in the light,
A spectacle to muse.

Balance sways with gentle grace,
As dark meets light's embrace,
Contrasting forces interlace,
An endless, shifting chase.

In the subtle interplay,
Of shadow, dark, and light,
Fluid contrasts come to play,
In soft and vibrant sight.

Dancing Shadows

In the dim glow of twilight's end,
Shadows rise to dance,
With every shape they twist and bend,
In quiet, dark romance.

The moonlight casts a silver stage,
For shadows to align,
In every corner, every page,
They move in silent rhyme.

Dark figures twirl in evening's breeze,
Their steps a whispered song,
In the company of ancient trees,
They find where they belong.

With every flicker, every sway,
Shadows trace their arc,
In the twilight's gentle play,
Like secrets in the dark.

As night descends, the dance goes on,
Shadows pirouette,
In the silence of the dawn,
Their presence won't forget.

In the Shadows

In the shadows where dreams reside.
Whispers of hope quietly glide.
Secrets hidden from prying eyes.
In the darkness, light softly tries.

Beneath the moon's soft, silver glow.
Paths unknown begin to show.
Echoes of laughter, joyous cries.
In the shadows, truth never lies.

Where fears are born and courage thrives.
In the silence, every soul strives.
Footsteps soft, unseen they tread.
In the shadows, whispers are fed.

Unity in Contrast

Colors clash in wild array.
Yet together, they make the day.
Opposites attract, as they say.
In contrast, unity finds its way.

Night meets day in twilight hue.
Sun and moon both share the view.
Dark and light, old and new.
In contrast, balance rings true.

Earth and sky, land and sea.
Different worlds, yet harmony.
Unity in diversity.
In contrast, life's symphony.

Silent Desires

Beneath the stars, wishes form.
In quiet hearts, they keep warm.
Unspoken dreams, passions swarm.
Silent desires, they transform.

In the stillness of the night.
Hopes and fears take quiet flight.
Yearnings hidden from the light.
Silent desires, out of sight.

Underneath the calm façade.
Longings persist, ever flawed.
In the silence, they applaud.
Silent desires, gently prodded.

The Strange and Beautiful

In the realm of the strange and odd.
Beauty blossoms, against the odds.
Nature's quirks, a visual nod.
The strange and beautiful applaud.

Wonders found in seas of blue.
Miracles formed in morning dew.
Oddities, but precious too.
The strange and beautiful renew.

Embrace the weird, the rare, the wild.
Cherish every wondrous child.
In every heart, beauty compiled.
The strange and beautiful, reconciled.

Two Ends of a Spectrum

In skies of dawn and dusk, we see,
Two worlds entwined in mystery.
One whispers dreams, the other sighs,
As sun and moon trade place, they rise.

Colors blend, then sharply part,
Creating shades, a painter's art.
From brightest hue to darkest night,
Their dance repeats, both soft and bright.

Light embraces shadows' grip,
In cosmic edge, they softly slip.
A meeting ground for night and day,
Where endless spectrums come to play.

In a spectrum's grand parade,
Boundaries blur, they softly fade.
Dualities in harmony,
In endless twirl, forever free.

The Silent River

A river flows through lands untamed,
In silence, whispers, softly named.
Its current tells a secret story,
Of time and life and fleeting glory.

Tranquil waters, softly glide,
Carrying tales, so quietly implied.
A mirror for the sky above,
Reflecting dreams and whispered love.

Banks adorned with nature's grace,
Listen close to its embrace.
Flowing onward, never still,
Its silent voice, a gentle thrill.

From mountain's heart to ocean's breast,
Through quietude, it finds its rest.
Passing life, both young and old,
The silent river, stories told.

Reflections in Twilight

Underneath the twilight's gleam,
Dreams emerge from day's last beam.
Reflections dance upon the tide,
As shadows lengthen, stars abide.

Colors fade to evening's hue,
Silver, gold, and dusky blue.
In these moments, hearts are free,
To wander near, yet silently.

Silent whispers fill the air,
As twilight answers every prayer.
Moonlight weaves its silver seam,
Through land of dusk and woven dream.

In twilight's glow, reflections bend,
Marking where the day will end.
A bridge between the night and day,
Where mysteries in shadows play.

A Dance of Shadows

On moonlit nights, the shadows rise,
To dance beneath the starlit skies.
Their forms take flight in eerie grace,
A whispered song to fill the space.

With every breeze, they twist and turn,
Shadows flicker, softly yearn.
They follow rhythms, hidden deep,
In silent dance, where dreams can sleep.

Upon the walls, their figures play,
A fleeting scene till break of day.
In the quiet, they unfold,
Stories of the night, untold.

Their dance is brief, yet timeless stays,
In memory, where moonlight sways.
A ballet cast in black and grey,
Ephemeral as dawn's first ray.

Contrasting Rhythms

In the serenade of night, stars gleam above,
Echoes whisper, the silence they disrupt,
A melody of moonlight, soft and refined,
While shadows dance, in rhythms undefined.

The dawn breaks forth with a golden hue,
Birds' symphonies as morning breaks anew,
Blending tunes of nature, sun-lit and bright,
Contrasting rhythms in the day's first light.

A river's flow, its currents twist and turn,
Against the rocks, murmurs in earnest churn,
Soothing discords in harmonic streams,
Contrasts merge in translucent dreams.

Life's patterns weave in oscillating flow,
Echoes of highs and lows in seamless row,
Unseen beauties in chaos interlace,
Contrasting rhythms find their place.

Boundless Unity

Across the sky, a robin's flight,
Unbounded realms, such pure delight,
Wings interwoven with the breeze,
Unity found in air, in trees.

Oceans merge, their waves overlap,
In salt and spray, no room for gap,
In vast expanse, the waters bind,
Boundless unity, ever intertwined.

Forests whisper in silent lore,
With leaves and roots, forevermore,
In nature's web, each thread aligns,
Boundless unity in verdant signs.

Day and night, in endless chase,
Shadow and light in boundless grace,
Eternal dance, with no divide,
Unity found on time's broad tide.

Entwined Fates

Two paths converge, in the twilight's gleam,
Whispered dreams and secret scheme,
Threaded lives in fate's embrace,
Bound by destiny's soft lace.

In the heartbeats' merged refrain,
Echoes of joy, depths of pain,
Stories written in the stars,
Fates entwined, leaving scars.

Held by choices, tender and harsh,
In the desert, and the marsh,
Entwined fates, weaves so tight,
Guided by both shadow and light.

One journey carved through the years,
Shared in laughter, shaped in tears,
Bound by love and sometimes hate,
Forever sealed, these entwined fates.

Opposite Pulses

Heartbeats echo in conflicting drums,
In silent caves or bustling slums,
Rhythms of life in varied beats,
Opposite pulses in crowded streets.

Winter's chill and summer's blaze,
Shifting seasons, time's great maze,
Cold and hot in endless play,
Opposite pulses guide their sway.

Harmony found in discord's song,
In right and wrong, where we belong,
Complementary yet diverse,
In one universe, opposites converse.

Silent nights and noisy days,
Linear paths in winding ways,
Yin and yang in life's broad sweep,
Opposite pulses in sync so deep.

The Other Side

A whisper in the willow's sway,
Beyond the fields of time.
We search for voices far away,
In realms of the sublime.

The moonlight casts a silver hue,
On pathways hidden deep.
We walk in dreams where shadows flew,
And ancient echoes sleep.

A bridge of stars, a cosmic thread,
Weaves tales of distant lands.
We cross the void, our spirits fed,
With light that understands.

The other side, a world unknown,
Yet closer than our breath.
In silent whispers, seeds are sown,
Transcending life and death.

Flickers of Connection

In moments, fleeting as a sigh,
Two hearts begin to blend.
Through whispered words, we find the tie,
An energy we lend.

A candle's flame, a distant glance,
Ignites the hidden spark.
In shared silence, we take the chance,
To navigate the dark.

An unspoken bond, soft and light,
Stronger than we perceive.
In every day, in every night,
In threads of fate, we weave.

Through life's mosaic, we align,
Our spirits interlace.
In flickers of connection, find,
A deep, abiding grace.

The Bridge Between

An arch of hope, from soul to soul,
We build with fragile care.
On gentle whispers, we extol,
An endless love laid bare.

With every step, the path unfolds,
A journey two embrace.
The bridge between, as twilight molds,
Our hearts in tender grace.

Beneath the sky, where dreams reside,
We cast our fears away.
In unity, we stride beside,
Through night and into day.

The bridge between our realms of thought,
A tapestry of dreams.
In every thread, the love we've sought,
In brilliant light, it beams.

Unseen Bonds

In silence, threads of fate entwine,
Invisible, yet strong.
Through space and time, in sacred lines,
They've held us all along.

Though eyes may miss, the heart will feel,
The ties that bind us close.
In subtle ways, they are revealed,
In laughter, tears, and hopes.

An unseen bond, like morning mist,
Embraces us each day.
In gentle love and quiet tryst,
We walk the heartfelt way.

These bonds, unseen, yet ever true,
In woven trust, they lie.
In every act, in every view,
Our souls are cast to fly.

Subtle Connections

Beneath the moon's soft silver sheen,
Whispers carry thoughts unseen,
Silent threads of heart and mind,
In quiet spaces, souls aligned.

The touch of breeze, a secret shared,
In the night's embrace, none compared,
Moments delicate, deeply felt,
Unspoken words where spirits melt.

Eyes that meet and dreams that blend,
Unknowing starts, peaceful ends,
Together in a timeless dance,
We find our way with subtle chance.

Quiet laughter, fleeting glance,
Fortunes crossed in space's expanse,
Each encounter, gentle sign,
Starlit paths to love divine.

From the stillness, wisdom flows,
In silent looks, our hearts disclose,
Mystic ties, forever bound,
In subtle connections, love is found.

Rising Together

Sunrise paints the sky anew,
Morning's whispers, fresh and true,
Hand in hand, we greet the day,
Together we will find our way.

With every dawn, a promise bright,
Shared dreams glowing in the light,
Through trials faced, we stand as one,
Stronger after all is done.

Life's ocean vast, its waves might roar,
Yet side by side, we'll reach the shore,
In unity, our strength reveals,
A power that no strife conceals.

Every heartbeat, echoing,
In harmony, our spirits sing,
A song of hope, of love so grand,
A future we will build, hand in hand.

As stars ignite the evening sky,
Under their gaze, we'll rise so high,
Together through the darkest night,
Our bond remains, forever bright.

Melding Spirits

In shadows cast by twilight's grace,
Two souls embark, a single space,
In moments where their thoughts entwine,
A melding spirits' grand design.

Passions whispered on the breeze,
Hearts that join in gentle ease,
The dance of life, of love's embrace,
In perfect sync, a tender trace.

With each shared laugh and quiet tear,
Their bond becomes more crystal clear,
In synchronicity, they find,
A harmony of heart and mind.

Eyes that speak in volumes grand,
Touch that calms, a steady hand,
United by an unseen thread,
A love deep as the words unsaid.

Through life's vast and winding course,
Together drawn by unseen force,
Melding spirits, hearts aligned,
In love's pure form, they're intertwined.

Different Shapes

Life's mosaic, bright and bold,
Different shapes and hues unfold,
Pieces varied, yet they blend,
In unity, our lives extend.

Each fragment tells a story true,
Unique perspectives, points of view,
Diverse paths that all converge,
Into a harmony, hearts emerge.

In every curve, in every line,
Beauty found in the design,
From differences, strength is born,
A tapestry that won't be torn.

Colors clash, yet complement,
Creating moments, heaven-sent,
Each shape brings its own light,
Together, they form purest sight.

In the grand mosaic of our days,
We find our way through life's arrays,
Different shapes in unity,
Crafting love's sweet symphony.

Unveiled Glances

Through shadowed lanes our paths entwine,
Beneath the arch of twilight's weave,
Unveiled glances, silent shrine,
In whispered secrets hearts believe.

Flickering hopes in moonlight bathed,
Soft-spoken dreams in night embraced,
Unseen yet felt, our spirits swayed,
In endless night, our fates are traced.

Beyond the veil of daylight's glare,
In realms untouched by time's long hand,
Hidden whispers, tender care,
Two souls' connection pure and grand.

Unveiled glances, moments fleet,
Yet linger on in memories deep,
Where heart and soul in silence meet,
A bond eternal, ours to keep.

Parallel Beat

Beneath one sky, two paths aligned,
In rhythm, hearts a steady drum,
Parallel beat, no ties confined,
In silent sync, together come.

One step apart, yet side by side,
With every pulse, a phrase composed,
Walking separate, yet stride for stride,
Our distant hearts in chorus posed.

In whispers soft, the night begins,
A symphony of silent beats,
Through star-lit dreams the music spins,
Two lives in concord, love's retreat.

In time's embrace, our echoes drape,
In tender waves, our hearts repeat,
In parallel, our fates reshape,
Two separate drums, a single beat.

Celestial Pair

In cosmic dance, two souls alight,
Amidst the stars, their love expands,
Celestial pair, in endless flight,
Through eons vast, they clasp their hands.

Their silken trails in darkness drawn,
A waltz of light, eternal bright,
The universe their stage at dawn,
In spheres of gold, they share the night.

Galaxies bow to their embrace,
In whispers soft, they carve the sky,
A tapestry of endless grace,
Two stars united, never shy.

Beyond the realms of mortal ties,
Eclipsed by none, their orbits share,
Through stellar winds and moonlit sighs,
They journey on, celestial pair.

Contrast in Harmony

In twilight's blend, where shadows kiss,
Their souls ignite with passion's spark,
Contrast in harmony, pure bliss,
In night's embrace, they leave their mark.

One heart of fire, one of ice,
Together forge an ageless dance,
In whispers soft, they pay the price,
For love's embrace in fleeting trance.

Where contrasts blend, they find recourse,
From friction, beauty softly springs,
A symphony in silent course,
Through tender notes, their spirit sings.

Their differences, a tapestry,
In woven strands of fate and time,
In contrast, find their destiny,
A bond unbroken, love's sweet rhyme.

Interlaced

Threads of fate: we intertwine,
Beneath the stars, our souls align.
In moonlit shadows, whispers play,
Guiding love through twilight's sway.

Hand in hand, we walk the night,
Casting dreams in silver light.
Time, a river, flows with grace,
Binding hearts in soft embrace.

Silent vows, eternal bond,
In your eyes, I see beyond.
Through highs and lows, we navigate,
Together, we challenge fate.

Moments linger, memories blend,
Love, our story with no end.
Interlaced, our spirits soar,
Evermore, we seek and explore.

Worlds Apart

Across the sea, beneath the sky,
Our hearts connect, though worlds away.
In silent dreams, we'll always fly,
In shadows of the break of day.

A whisper in the howling wind,
Carries our love through distance vast.
Despite the miles, our spirits blend,
In memories of all things past.

The stars above, our secret guide,
Illuminate the paths we tread.
Though oceans wide, we can't divide,
The bond in words we never said.

Night and day, in shift and change,
Our hearts beat with an endless pull.
Worlds apart, yet love's exchange,
Keeps our destiny hopeful.

Fusion of Echoes

Whispers from the ages past,
Echo through this hallowed hall.
A symphony that's built to last,
Voices blend and spirits call.

Timeless tunes, a blended song,
From heart to heart, we find our place.
Echoes linger, soft yet strong,
Connecting us in warm embrace.

Memory and dream unite,
In a dance both old and new.
Fusion of the day's twilight,
Painting skies with sunset hues.

Across the void, through nights we chase,
Echoes of the love we knew.
Joined in infinite embrace,
We blend as one, forever true.

Heartstrings Align

In the quiet of the dawn,
Where the morning whispers lie.
Heartstrings play a tender song,
Beneath the painted sky.

Every glance, a story told,
Every touch, a promise deep.
In your arms, warmth enfolds,
In your love, my soul does sleep.

Life's a dance of joy and pain,
Yet together, we are strong.
Through the sun, the wind, the rain,
Our hearts beat a timeless song.

With each moment, love refines,
In the symphony divine.
Through our gaze, the world aligns,
Bound together, heartstrings intertwine.

Silent Sparks

In the hush of twilight's fall,
Where shadows softly creep,
Silent sparks ignite the night,
In dreams we gently seep.

Whispers ride the evening breeze,
Stars alight in silent flare,
A dance of light in muted grace,
Secrets held high in the air.

Through the veil of endless dark,
Silent sparks of hope unwind,
Guiding hearts with quiet glow,
In their luminescent bind.

Beneath the canopy of night,
Silent thoughts like embers cast,
In the realm where dreams convene,
Silent sparks, a gentle blast.

Infinite beyond the eye,
Silent sparks in cosmic flight,
In their glow, a silent vow,
To guard the dreams of night.

Pastel Dreams

With hues of morning softly spread,
Pastel dreams upon us lay,
A canvas painted by the dawn,
In tender, muted play.

Colors blend in whispered tones,
A symphony of light,
Dreams of pastel gently wove,
In the tapestry of night.

Blossoms bloom in gentle shades,
A cascade soft and bright,
In fields where pastel dreams reside,
They dance until first light.

Through the mist of early hours,
Pastel dreams take gentle flight,
Gliding on the morning breeze,
Into the arms of light.

In the quietude of dawn,
Pastel dreams unfurl and sigh,
A world awash in tender hues,
Where tranquil thoughts can lie.

Vast Affections

Amid the sea of endless skies,
Vast affections freely roam,
Heartfelt whispers, boundless waves,
A love in endless tome.

Beneath the realms of starry night,
Affections vast and wide,
In every glimmer, every shine,
Eternal ties abide.

Through time and space, they journey on,
Affections vast and true,
In every heartbeat, every breath,
A timeless bond shines through.

In the tapestry of life,
Vast affections intertwine,
We weave a story rich and deep,
With love both yours and mine.

Across the sky, across the earth,
Affections vast will soar,
A testament to love's embrace,
Forever, evermore.

Two As One

In the quiet of the heart,
Two as one, our souls unite,
Bound by threads unseen but strong,
In love's eternal light.

In the dance of life we move,
Two as one, our steps align,
Harmony in every breath,
Together we define.

Through the trials that we face,
Two as one, we stand and fight,
Hand in hand we journey forth,
Through the darkest night.

In the whisper of the wind,
Two as one, we find our way,
Guided by a love so pure,
In each and every day.

In the song of life we sing,
Two as one, our voices blend,
A melody of endless love,
Together, till the end.

Divergent Paths

At the crossroads where we stand,
Two roads diverge, hand in hand,
One path leads to dawn's embrace,
The other, starry night's chase.

Steps we take, sure but hesitant,
Dreams unfold, often resistant,
With every turn, choices vast,
Future blends with echoes past.

Whispers of the breeze do guide,
Nature's signs will not divide,
Though we walk on different trails,
Endless unity prevails.

Distance stretches but hearts unite,
Persevere through darkest night,
Journeys end as whispers blend,
In twilight, our paths descend.

Choices mark our footprints deep,
Memories for us to keep,
Paths diverge yet intertwined,
In life's scroll, our fate defined.

Infinite Bonds

Threads unseen, bonds of light,
Binding souls, pure and bright,
Infinite, our spirits meet,
Love's embrace, hearts complete.

Time and space may drift apart,
Here remains a woven heart,
Lines unseen but ever strong,
Linking notes to timeless song.

Moments pass, years unfold,
Silver strands weave tales untold,
In the silence, whispers share,
Echoes of a love rare.

Even in the storm's loud cry,
Undying, our spirits fly,
In the tapestry we find,
Connections of a kind mind.

Infinite, the bond does glow,
In the depth of starry flow,
Through the ages, bonds will grow,
Love's true essence, we both know.

Hidden Harmony

In the silence, secrets hum,
Hidden tales of what will come,
Nature's symphony, softly played,
In the shadows, whispers made.

Leaves do rustle, secrets told,
Mysteries in its fold,
Sing the song of hidden peace,
In the calm, worry's release.

Barely heard, the heart's refrain,
Love in shadows to remain,
Hidden notes in silent air,
Softly sing, beyond compare.

Echoes fade, yet linger on,
In the dawn's first gentle yawn,
In the quiet, we will find,
Harmony of the kind mind.

Silent hallows, whispers drift,
In the stillness, hearts uplift,
Nature's whisper, soft and true,
Hidden harmony, I find in you.

Silent Affections

In the quiet of the night,
Lies a love, gentle and light,
Unspoken words, emotions pure,
In the silence, we find our cure.

Eyes do speak without a sound,
In their depth, feelings found,
Silent glances, love does share,
Moments held in tender care.

Touches brief, yet deeply felt,
In your warmth, my heart does melt,
Gentle gestures, whispered vows,
In serenity, love allows.

Echoes of a silent song,
In your presence, I belong,
Unheard symphonies, love's tune,
In silence, our hearts commune.

Without words, affection grows,
In the stillness, love bestows,
Silent bonds that ever shine,
In your eyes, forever mine.

Between the Lines

In silence, whispers softly lay
Where words unsaid begin to play
A dance of thoughts, subtle, unseen
Between the lines, dreams intervene

Shadows form in twilight's grace
Hints of truth, an unseen trace
A language forged of silent binds
Unfolds where heart and soul entwine

Hidden meanings drift on air
Secrets shared without despair
In the quiet, truths align
Stories told between the lines

Moonlit nights reveal the code
In the spaces, paths are strode
A symphony of silent signs
Speaks volumes in between the lines

Through the whispers, find the key
Unlock the worlds that cannot be
In the echoes, hear designs
Concealed within, between the lines

Echoes of Us

Between the echoes of the past
In shadows long, our memories last
A whisper from a distant place
The echoes of us, time can't erase

A moment caught in twilight's glint
Our laughter like a faint imprint
Across the years, through dusk and dawn
The echoes of our love live on

Through whispered winds and gentle sighs
Our story lingers, never dies
In every breath, in every pause
The echoes of us, without a cause

The world may change, the days move fast
Yet in the silence, we are cast
Reflections found in moon's soft glow
The echoes of us always show

In dreams they speak, in hush they stay
Reminders of a far-off day
Forever bound, through time they thrust
The whispers of the echoes of us

Divergent Paths

Two roads diverged within our view
Each path a choice, a journey new
One led to where the sun does shine
The other, shadows intertwine

We stood at crossroads, weighed the cost
With every step, direction lost
Yet in our hearts, a compass stayed
To guide us through each night's charade

One path may lead to joy untamed
Another, sorrow lightly named
Yet just as rivers bend and weave
Our paths converge, and then they leave

With every choice, a story spins
Of where we've been and what begins
The journey shaped by fleeting drafts
In every step, divergent paths

So with each turn, embrace the call
Whether we rise or gently fall
In life's design, the aftermath
Is crafted by divergent paths

Whispers in the Night

Beneath the stars, in crescent light
There come the whispers in the night
Softly spoken, secrets shared
In silent realms, our souls are bared

The breeze carries tales untold
Of love and loss, both new and old
Each sigh a story, whispered slight
A tender song of whispered night

Moonlight dances on the leaves
Cradling dreams that night conceives
In shadows deep, in hues of white
Lie whispers of the silent night

Through the veil of midnight's calm
Hear the echoes of a distant psalm
A serenade, a heart's delight
The whispers of an endless night

In the quiet, truth takes flight
Guided by the soft starlight
Yet as dawn breaks, fades the sight
Of whispers only found in night

Temporal Ties

Moments flash like fireflies
In the tapestry of time
Memories carved in the skies
In a fleeting, silent rhyme

Present, past, and future blend
Threads of life that intertwine
Messages that fate does send
Woven lines that so define

Sands of time drift through our grasp
Echoes of the days gone by
In temporal ties, we clasp
Whispered breaths of a soft sigh

Journeys vast, with hearts we roam
Over oceans, through the night
Drawn by ties that lead us home
Guided by the morning light

Time's relentless steady flow
Carves its path with gentle ease
Through seasons it will bestow
Memories cast on the breeze

Eternal Embrace

In the quiet of the night
Stars bear witness to our love
Endless as their silver flight
Shining from the skies above

Hearts entwined in timeless dance
Whispered secrets held so dear
A vow sealed at fate's first glance
Blossoming with every tear

Endless tides and moonlit waves
Gentle touch of destiny
Finding solace that it craves
In an endless, boundless sea

Souls that weave a sacred lace
Through the realms of time and space
Held in the eternal embrace
Of a love we can't erase

Every breath an ode divine
Every heartbeat, love's sweet sign
Eternal, this pledge of mine
Until stars cease their bright shine

Silent Symphonies

In the hush of dawn's first light
Nature's whispers say hello
Melodies that fill the night
In a gentle ebb and flow

Leaves that rustle in the wind
Crickets' serenades so fine
Silent symphonies begin
Underneath the swaying pines

Ripples dance upon the brook
Raindrops play a soft refrain
Symphonies in every nook
Nature's ever gentle strain

Moonlight's soft, enchanting glow
Guides the river's quiet song
In these moments, we do know
Where our hearts and souls belong

Silent notes, a hidden tale
In the rustling of the leaves
Nature's music will prevail
In the air that weaves and breathes

Alternate Realms

In dreams, we cross the boundary line
To realms where fantasies unwind
Unknown paths in moon's own shine
Boundless worlds of another kind

Alternate realms where shadows play
Mysteries wrap their woven dance
Beyond the light of day
Roaming free in chance's trance

Castles in the skies we roam
Mystic forests, lush and deep
Find in magic our new home
Through the veil of dreams we leap

Stars align in cosmic art
Guiding through each astral maze
Connection felt, though we're apart
In alternate realms' haze

In whispers of a differing sphere
Secrets glow, unseen, unfound
Realms that feel so crystal clear
Yet where we tread no footprints bound

Echoes of Us

In whispers of a time long past,
An echo sings, it does not fade,
Through corridors that memories cast,
Our shadows dance, in twilight's shade.

A love that whispers secrets new,
In murmurs soft, yet clear as glass,
The echoes speak, a story true,
Where time and space they gently pass.

Through fleeting moments, swift and sweet,
Our hearts converge in silent trust,
In echoes, old and new, we meet,
Forever bound, as if we must.

Unseen by eyes, but heard by soul,
The echoes weave our tale of gold,
Together, we make the whole,
A story shared, forever told.

Hearts in Collision

In cosmic tides, our hearts align,
A clash of stars, a burst of flame,
Your eyes meet mine, a sacred sign,
In chaos wild, we play love's game.

Through worlds apart, yet souls collide,
An astral dance, a stellar grace,
In every beat, our truths reside,
Two hearts, one space, in love's embrace.

A fiery touch, a warm caress,
The universe in tangled strings,
In every pause, in every press,
Eternity within us rings.

In the collision, sparks ignite,
A tapestry of scars and bliss,
In every beat, our hearts recite,
A timeless tale penned with a kiss.

Unseen Connections

Beyond the veil of what's been seen,
Lies threads of gold, too fine to break,
In whispers light and shadows keen,
A bond is formed, no force can shake.

In silent ways our paths entwine,
Unheard by ear, but felt by heart,
Invisible, yet so divine,
Unseen threads play their secret part.

Through dreams and thoughts, connections bloom,
A tapestry of fates unspun,
In every silence, there is room,
For unseen ties from heart to one.

Though eyes may search, they may not find,
These bonds that lie beneath the veil,
Yet heart to heart and mind to mind,
In quiet tones, our spirits sail.

Parallel Dreams

In realms where shadows dance with light,
Our dreams run parallel and deep,
Through twilight, dawn, and silent night,
In whispered waves across we sweep.

Two worlds that walk a mirrored path,
Unseen by those with eyes awake,
In dreams we find each other's laugh,
And twilight's brush our fears does break.

A night where moon and sun may meet,
And stars reflect our hidden themes,
Our hearts, in secret, softly beat,
In tandem with parallel dreams.

Though space and time may stand apart,
In slumber's weave we come alive,
Across the veil, from heart to heart,
In dreams, together we arrive.

Under the Surface

Beneath the waves in silent grace,
Lies a world unseen to the eyes.
Secrets whisper in hidden place,
Where the ocean's mystery lies.

Shadows dance with fish and stone,
In caves where light dares not to roam.
Whispers echo from the unknown,
Revealing dreams lost from home.

Currents weave a tale untold,
Of treasures hid, both dark and cold.
Yet in the deep, stories unfold,
Narrating histories of the bold.

Nature's song, a fluid ballet,
Moves in rhythm, night and day.
Under waves, where secrets stay,
Life's unseen, in tranquil sway.

In depths where sunlight cannot trace,
Exists a realm in quiet embrace.
There, life's art finds its space,
Under the surface, void of haste.

Fractures of Time

Across the sky, the stars align,
Through cracks in life's fragile design.
Moments whisper, then unwind,
In fractures of time, we define.

A clock's soft tick, an ancient rhyme,
Echoes through the halls of prime.
History and present intertwine,
In the fractures, threads combine.

Memories dance, a twinkling light,
Shimmering in the darkest night.
Within the fractures, hopes ignite,
Guiding hearts when lost from sight.

Days slip by, as grains of sand,
In time's grasp, we try to stand.
Yet in each fracture, a gentle hand,
Reminds us of life's grand command.

Through the fractures, love persists,
In whispered moments, it exists.
A tapestry of held-long trysts,
In broken time, our lives kissed.

A Silent Song

In the stillness of the morn,
Where dreams are gently born,
A silent song begins to form,
Carried by the breeze, still warm.

No words to break this delicate tune,
Just whispers of the rustling dune.
Nature's choir, a blessing boon,
Underneath the timeless moon.

Leaves that rustle, waves that sigh,
Breath of wind, a soft reply.
Silent song, it drifts on high,
Through the vast and endless sky.

In this quiet, hearts find peace,
Worries and fears begin to cease.
The silent song, a sweet release,
Caressing souls with gentle ease.

In every dawn, this song persists,
An ode to life, it silently insists.
A melody that time resists,
In silence, endless beauty exists.

The Unspoken Pulse

There's a beat that lives within,
A pulse of love, unseen but keen.
In hearts it sings, a vibrant hymn,
The unspoken pulse serene.

When words fall short, and silence reigns,
This pulse endures, it never wanes.
It bridges gaps, it soothes the pains,
In rhythms, love's essence sustains.

The breath between each spoken word,
Carries more than what's been heard.
In the stillness, it's inferred,
By the heartbeats gently stirred.

Emotions flow in unseen streams,
In quiet moments, hopes and dreams.
The unspoken pulse redeems,
Gifting life its gentle gleams.

In solitude, in crowds alike,
It travels on, it takes no hike.
The unspoken pulse, nature's strike,
Binding souls in love's soft spike.

Parallel Heartbeats

In the quiet of night, two hearts beat as one,
A rhythm so gentle, like whispers in the dark.
Across distant lands under the same bright sun,
Connected by dreams, sharing one cosmic spark.

Though miles may separate, the bond remains true,
In stories untold, felt in the silent air.
Two souls on a journey, forever renew,
Parallel heartbeats in a timeless affair.

Each echoing pulse, a promise so deep,
A dance in the shadows, a secret to keep.
In moments apart, together in thought,
A love everlasting, forever unsought.

From dawn unto dusk, in twilight's embrace,
They wander together, in infinite space.
A beat intertwined, an invisible line,
Parallel heartbeats, forever in time.

A World Between

In a world between dreams and the waking day,
Where shadows of yesteryears softly sway.
There lies a realm where lost loves stay,
In whispers of dusk, they come out to play.

Memories float on the edge of night,
Draped in hues of pale starlight.
Whispers of futures not yet seen,
In this world that bridges the serene.

Here ambitions are born of twilight's grace,
Merging the past's touch with future's embrace.
In sweet repose, where hopes convene,
Lives the gentle spirit of the in-between.

A refuge for minds that wander afar,
Guided by the softest northern star.
In a world between reality's sheen,
Angels and mortals share the same dream.

Where time suspends its unyielding pace,
And dreams meet truth in a tender place.
A world between the seen and unseen,
Lingers forever, a mystical sheen.

Chords of Distance

In the quiet of night, the chords gently play,
Notes of love across the vast expanse.
A melody of longing, hearts far away,
Connected by strings in a rhythmic dance.

The distance between, an ocean so wide,
Yet music unites the hearts it guides.
Each note a step on this journey apart,
A symphony of love from the depth of the heart.

In the silence, the chords whisper sweet,
Songs of love in every heartbeat.
Though miles divide, the music remains,
Binding together hearts and their pains.

As the moonlight bathes the world in glow,
The chords of distance ebb and flow.
In every echo, a promise is found,
The distance fades with every sound.

A serenade of hope in each refrain,
Love's tender chord conquers the pain.
Across the divide, through the silent mist,
The chords of distance forever persist.

An Invisible Thread

An invisible thread connects two hearts,
Unseen by eyes but felt deep within.
Through time and distance, it never departs,
A bond unbroken, where love does begin.

In the silence of dawn, or the hush of night,
This thread weaves stories of joy and pain.
It binds souls tight, in the softest light,
An eternal promise in an endless chain.

Though words may fail and miles may spread,
Love's thread remains ever so true.
In moments apart, this bond is fed,
By memories shared, and dreams anew.

Invisible yet unyielding, its strength endured,
Through trials and tears, it stands secure.
An unspoken vow, so tender and pure,
This thread of love is life's grand tour.

Woven with care, from spirit's finest fiber,
Each heart connected, a devoted subscriber.
An invisible thread, forever unfurled,
Binding together two souls in this world.

The Space of Hope

In the night, where dreams take flight,
Beyond the stars, where wishes alight,
A realm unfolds, both vast and bright,
The space of hope, an endless sight.

Through cosmic waves, our spirits soar,
Past galaxies, to distant shore,
In whispers soft, we yearn for more,
For futures aglow, like tales of yore.

Each twinkling star, a beacon's plea,
A guide for souls, to set them free,
In constellations, we seek to see,
A glimpse of all we hope to be.

In stellar winds, our hopes entwine,
In timeless dance, to fate we'll bind,
Beneath the skies, so vast, divine,
In space of hope, our hearts align.

With every dream, a spark of light,
In shadows deep, it shines so bright,
Through endless dark, it fuels the fight,
The space of hope, our souls' delight.

Of Stars and Silence

In the quiet, where whispers pause,
Beneath the night, with all its laws,
A symphony of silent cause,
Of stars and silence, nature's clause.

The heavens speak without a sound,
In shimmering lights, so profound,
A cosmic dance, where dreams are found,
In silence deep, our hearts are bound.

Each star, a tale of ancient lore,
Of worlds unknown, and thoughts explore,
In silence vast, they teach us more,
Of mysteries held at the core.

In stillness, we find space to dream,
A tranquil realm, where hopes redeem,
Of stars and silence, a gentle theme,
A lullaby in night's soft gleam.

Through quiet breaths, our spirits fly,
To distant realms, beyond the sky,
Of stars and silence, a boundless tie,
That connects the soul to the eye.

Silent Symphony

In forests deep, where shadows play,
A silent symphony holds sway,
In nature's choir, the spirits stay,
In whispered notes, they find their way.

The rustling leaves, a soft refrain,
A melody without a name,
In every breeze, a gentle claim,
The silent symphony, fierce yet tame.

The moonlight casts, a silver streak,
On whispering waters, cool and sleek,
In stillness vast, the night does speak,
A symphony for those who seek.

In every dawn, a fresh debut,
The morning mist, a hazy hue,
The silent symphony, pure and true,
A quiet tune the heart pursues.

In solitude, we hear it best,
A song of peace, a call to rest,
In nature's arms, we're truly blessed,
The silent symphony, a gentle jest.

Paths Not Crossed

In life we tread, through lanes unknown,
On winding roads, where seeds are sown,
Of dreams and paths, we walk alone,
Paths not crossed, yet not our own.

Each step we take, a choice we make,
On trails we forge, or paths we break,
In silence, wander, for our sake,
In life's vast web, the chance we take.

Of meetings lost, in time's embrace,
Of unknown hands, and unseen face,
Of fleeting shadows, we can't trace,
Paths not crossed, leave empty space.

Through every turn, a door might close,
A missed connection, yet who knows,
What lies beyond, where life just flows,
On paths not crossed, our journey grows.

In reflection, we might ponder,
What could have been, and often wonder,
Yet in each step, we grow fonder,
Of paths we've chosen, and their thunder.

Varied Hues

In twilight's glow of purple skies,
Where crimson dreams and visions rise.
The golden sun bids day's adieu,
Your face I see in varied hues.

Emerald leaves in summer's dance,
With sapphire lakes in pure expanse.
Amber grains beneath our feet,
In varied hues, our souls retreat.

Cerulean waves caress the shore,
With gentle whispers, evermore.
Obsidian night in velvet's guise,
In varied hues, the world complies.

Scarlet blooms in fields so vast,
Memories painted by the past.
Ochre trails where hearts diffuse,
In varied hues, our paths choose.

Seasons meld as time unfolds,
Stories in the hues we've told.
With every shade, a life imbues,
In varied hues, our love renews.

Fragmented Unity

In shards of glass, reflections lie,
Each piece a truth beneath the sky.
A broken whole can still unite,
In fragmented unity, we find light.

Through fractured lines, the world collides,
Yet beauty in the cracks abides.
Separate hearts in common plea,
In fragmented unity, we are free.

Torn apart by fate's cruel hand,
Together, yet alone we stand.
Mosaic lives arranged in glee,
In fragmented unity, we see.

Singular paths with destinies crossed,
Finding love in what seemed lost.
Chaos binds us seamlessly,
In fragmented unity, we agree.

Though divided, we conspire,
To build our dreams, to lift us higher.
One vision shared collectively,
In fragmented unity, we'll be.

Shifting Tides

Beneath the moon's ethereal glow,
The shifting tides of oceans flow.
Our love, like waves, ebbs and swells,
In shifting tides, our story tells.

Upon the shore, where souls embrace,
Eternal dance in fluid grace.
Rhythmic push and gentle pull,
In shifting tides, the world is full.

Secrets whispered by the sea,
In waves, our hopes come to be.
With each tide a chance to start,
In shifting tides, we find our heart.

Tempest winds may fiercely roar,
Yet calm will come to still the shore.
Resilient souls in changing stride,
In shifting tides, we will abide.

Through rising crests and valleys low,
Together, hand in hand, we'll go.
Constant love as waters guide,
In shifting tides, we shall confide.

Mirrored Souls

In silvered glass, our spirits meet,
Mirrored souls reflect complete.
Through crystal panes, our eyes behold,
A love untold, our destinies unfold.

Two hearts entwined in perfect sync,
Gazing deep beyond the brink.
Mirrored lives encased in time,
Our harmony, a silent chime.

Echoes of a shared past blend,
In mirrors, love has no end.
Parallel paths fate weaves and molds,
Mirrored souls, a story told.

Light and shadow, juxtapose,
In reflections, affection grows.
One soul split in two to find,
Mirrored halves, forever kind.

Through polished glass, our dreams align,
Mirrored souls in love's design.
Bound by fate and cosmic roles,
Eternal dance of mirrored souls.

Uncharted Affection

In the realm where hearts gently tread,
Uncharted paths by emotions are led,
Soft whispers of love call and spread,
Lines of fate in tender hues are read.

Eyes meet in the twilight's embrace,
Shared glances weave a delicate lace,
Fragile dreams with hope interlace,
A silent vow, time cannot erase.

Invisible strings our spirits bind,
Love's symphony plays in our mind,
In hidden corners, true warmth we find,
A cherished secret, undefined.

Amidst the stars, feelings take flight,
Illuminated by the moon's soft light,
A journey begun in the still of night,
Hearts navigate, pure and bright.

Beyond words, past written bounds,
Where the essence of affection resounds,
Infinite are the connections it surrounds,
In the uncharted, true love is found.

The Space Between

In the silence of words unspoken,
Lies a space where thoughts are broken,
Whispers float, bonds remain unbroken,
Silent threads by souls are woven.

In the pauses, our hearts converse,
Silent tales and secrets traverse,
Between the lines, emotions immerse,
Distance shrinks, becoming terse.

Stars shine in the quiet sky,
Illuminating where feelings lie,
In the space that makes us sigh,
Unseen tears and laughter fly.

A silent dance in twilight's grace,
No need for time or empty space,
Shared moments, love's embrace,
Speaking in the interstices face to face.

No barrier, just a tender seam,
Binding souls in a delicate dream,
In the narrow, threads esteem,
The space between is more than it may seem.

Harmony and Discord

In the tapestry of life's song,
Harmony and discord belong,
Intertwined, where we find,
The strength to grow, our voices strong.

Chords of laughter, notes of pain,
A melody in the sunshine and rain,
Together they form life's refrain,
A symphony that won't wane.

In the clash and in the peace,
In moments of pure release,
We find ourselves, a sweet caprice,
The dance of life will never cease.

Unity and division blend,
In every curve and every bend,
A perfect harmony they send,
Tales of conflict, love to mend.

In balance, our spirits soar,
Merged are harmony and discord,
Creating bonds, forevermore,
Together, we unlock life's door.

Unspoken Yearning

In the heart's quiet chamber lies,
A yearning hidden from prying eyes,
Soft whispers of desires arise,
Beneath the veil of twilight skies.

Beneath the calm, emotions churn,
In silence, passions twist and turn,
For the warmth, the soul does yearn,
A burning flame, unconcerned.

Eyes reveal what lips conceal,
A silent story, deep and real,
Words unsaid, their secrets reveal,
A love unvoiced, hearts feel.

In dreams, the truths we chase,
In longing's delicate embrace,
Unspoken is the tender case,
Yearning transcends time and space.

Silent wishes, a lover's plea,
In shadows cast by twilight's tree,
Unvoiced bonds set the heart free,
Yearning for what is meant to be.

On Separate Shores

Across the waves, a silent plea
Two hearts that beat in unity
Yet distance grows, an aching sore
Together now on separate shores

Whispers carried on the breeze
Memories that never cease
Ocean's depths can't drown the lore
Two souls adrift on separate shores

Gazing up, the same night's sky
Holds the dreams we can't deny
Wishing stars could bridge the pore
To end our time on separate shores

In the quiet of the night
Moonlight's touch, a soft, faint light
We endure and long for more
Love persists on separate shores

And though apart, our spirits soar
In timeless dance forevermore
For the heart, there's no marked drawer
Where we belong, not separate shores

The Mirror's Edge

Upon the edge, reflections merge
Where dreams and fears begin to surge
A mirrored world in silent pledge
Truth revealed on mirror's edge

Shadows play in twinkling light
Echoes of the endless night
Answers found in hidden wedge
Mysteries at the mirror's edge

Eyes that peer into the glass
See the future, see the past
Wisdom waits by whispered hedge
Life unfolds on mirror's edge

Guard the secrets, keep them tight
Hold the gaze till morning's light
Journey through the mind's vast sledge
To find the self at mirror's edge

Each insight gained, a subtle nudge
Spirit grows and thoughts won't budge
Reflected depths, we cannot hedge
Truth embraced on mirror's edge

Eternal Parallel

Two paths that run but never meet
Parallel lines, each step discreet
Yet in the silence, they can tell
A shared journey, eternal parallel

Both see the sun, both touch the sky
Feel the breeze as days go by
Walkers stride with tales to knell
Lives aligned in eternal parallel

Though the space between is vast
Memories and dreams hold fast
Kindred spirits break the shell
Connecting in eternal parallel

Stars above and roots below
Guide the paths where souls will go
Unified, though none can tell
The promise of eternal parallel

In each heart, an endless thread
Unseen ties that go unsaid
For in this bond, we will dwell
Forever in eternal parallel

Boundless through Barriers

Walls may rise, intentions clear
Limits drawn by doubt and fear
Yet courage steps where borders steer
Boundless hearts through barriers sheer

Chains that bind can't hold the dream
Through cracks of light, the hope will stream
Strength no obstacle can shear
Boundless love through barriers near

Minds set free by thoughts profound
Break the silence, shatter ground
In the face of limits, cheer
Boundless spirit through barriers here

Hands that hold through every trial
Hearts that leap o'er every mile
Bound together, year by year
Boundless life through barriers dear

Distance, time, nor fate's design
Will not split what's truly twine
For triumph rings in hearts sincere
Boundless through all barriers clear

Fleeting Glances

In crowded rooms, across the way,
Our eyes would meet, then dart astray.
A silent dance, a shy ballet,
In fleeting glances, hearts convey.

Through bustling streets, you catch my sight,
A moment shared in daylight's bite.
Our unspoken stories ignite,
In fleeting glances, trust takes flight.

In coffee shops, in market stalls,
A wordless whisper through the walls.
Our gazes locked, the world enthralls,
In fleeting glances, love befalls.

At sunset's glow, as shadows form,
A passing look both soft and warm.
We write our own, untold reform,
In fleeting glances, hearts transform.

In moonlit nights, beneath the stars,
An echo from a world afar.
We are what all these moments are,
In fleeting glances, we unbar.

Invisible Strings

Threads unseen, yet tightly bound,
In whispered winds, our souls are found.
A silent song, a sacred sound,
Invisible strings, our hearts profound.

Through restless nights and dreamy days,
In subtle cues and quiet ways.
We navigate the starry maze,
Invisible strings, our bond portrays.

Across the miles, under moon's glow,
Our spirits dance, though winds may blow.
Through every high, through every low,
Invisible strings, our love does show.

Beyond the sight, beyond the touch,
In every word, we say so much.
An unseen force that means so much,
Invisible strings, a gentle clutch.

In moments lost, in timeless gleam,
We trace the path of every dream.
Together in this endless stream,
Invisible strings, our endless theme.

The Uncharted Soul

In realms unmarked, where spirits soar,
A journey starts, an open door.
Through depths unknown and tales of lore,
The uncharted soul, forevermore.

With courage bold and heart on fire,
To seek the truth and still aspire.
In shadows cold or sun's desire,
The uncharted soul shall not tire.

Through forests dense and oceans wide,
In every tear and every tide.
With dreams to chase, with love as guide,
The uncharted soul walks with pride.

No map to chart the winding road,
Yet light within will ease the load.
To distant lands, where peace is sowed,
The uncharted soul, a fervent ode.

In whispers soft, in roaring call,
Through rise and fall, the soul stands tall.
Embrace the void, embrace it all,
The uncharted soul will not stall.

Reflections and Ripples

In water's face, my thoughts do dwell,
A mirrored world with tales to tell.
In ripples born from silence fell,
Reflections cast by nature's spell.

A pebble tossed, a secret shared,
Its waves expand, a message bared.
In every ripple, love is aired,
Reflections of a heart that dared.

Beneath the sun, beneath the shade,
In fleeting shapes, our hearts are laid.
In every hue and every grade,
Reflections and ripples are portrayed.

By moonlit lakes, in twilight's gleam,
Our dreams unfold, like silver streams.
In silent bursts and whispered beams,
Reflections hold our hopes and dreams.

In stillness found, in gentle sway,
A journey told in liquid play.
In every night, in every day,
Reflections and ripples light our way.

Wings of Serendipity

In the silence of the morning light,
Serendipity takes its flight.
Through the mist and through the haze,
A chance transformed, a life amazed.

Whispers of the unseen breeze,
Carry hopes among the trees.
Paths we took, so unforeseen,
Lending grace to moments in between.

Labyrinths of fate unwind,
Serendipity, our kind guide.
Leading hearts where dreams reside,
In twilight's tender, tranquil tide.

Boundless skies, a canvas wide,
On wings of chance, is where we glide.
Ephemeral as the morning dew,
Serendipity, so pure and true.

Embrace the flow of life's delight,
In its dance, we find our light.
Wings of serendipity, take flight,
Into the heart of endless night.

A Heart Unseen

In shadows deep where secrets lay,
There beats a heart, so gracious, brave.
Encased in quiet, unseen grace,
It lights the dark, a warm embrace.

Beneath the surface calm and still,
Lives a spirit, strong of will.
Silent whispers fill the void,
A heart unseen, yet life enjoyed.

No chains can bind its boundless song,
In realms where only it belongs.
Through whispered woods and fallen leaves,
A heart unseen, its own bequeaths.

Beneath the stars in endless skies,
It dreams and dances, never dies.
A symphony of silent screams,
A heart unseen can chase its dreams.

As moons wax and wane again,
In love and loss, unseen remains.
A heart unseen, forever free,
Dwells where no eye can ever see.

Beyond the Horizon

Where the sky meets the endless blue,
Dreams unfold and hearts renew.
Beyond the edge of sight and sound,
Lies a world, where hope is found.

Waves that dance in twilight's glow,
Carry secrets, tales of old.
Far beyond the horizon's reach,
Magic whispers in the speech.

In the cusp of dawn and dusk,
The soul finds solace, sheds its husk.
Beyond the rim of dawn's first light,
Endless wonders, pure delight.

Stars align in cosmic dance,
Guiding destinies, blessed by chance.
Beyond the veil of time and space,
Awaits a realm of boundless grace.

Trust the tides to guide your way,
Through the night into the day.
Beyond the horizon's line,
Lies a destiny divine.

Threads of Us

Interwoven, strands of time,
Threads of us, in silent rhyme.
Tapestry of lives entwined,
In every stitch, a story shines.

In the warp and weft of years,
Joy and sorrow, hopes and fears.
Each connection sewn with care,
Binding hearts beyond repair.

Colors dance in vivid streams,
Woven with our silent dreams.
A fabric strong, yet made of trust,
The intricate threads of us.

Memories faded, yet not lost,
In the loom, no matter the cost.
Every twist and turn creates,
A tapestry that love awaits.

Hold the threads, do not let go,
For in each lies love's gentle glow.
In the fabric of our days,
Threads of us forever stay.

The Veil and the Light

In twilight's gentle, soft embrace,
Where shadows dance, the stars give chase,
A mystic veil, both dark and bright,
Unfurls beneath the endless night.

Mysteries whisper on the breeze,
As moonlight filters through the trees,
In realms where dreams and silence blend,
The line between, we're left to mend.

Through whispered winds, our spirits roam,
In search of twilight's fleeting home,
Where veil and light, in tender seam,
Are woven with our deepest dreams.

In every shadow, light does play,
And darkness too must have its say,
For in this dance of bright and shade,
The heart's true path is gently laid.

So walk the line of night and dawn,
In twilight's truth, we are reborn,
Embrace the veil, embrace the light,
For in their union, find your sight.

Stars in the Abyss

Within the deep abyss of night,
Where velvet shadows snuff the light,
A million stars, like diamonds, gleam,
Each one a whisper of a dream.

The cosmos sings its silent song,
A symphony we've known so long,
In depths where darkness holds its reign,
The stars remind, through joy and pain.

Eternal, steady, bright, and true,
In night's embrace, they shine anew,
Against the black, their sparkle pure,
Their light, our anchor to ensure.

From depths unfathomable, wide,
These stars our guiding spirits guide,
Through chaos vast, through void so still,
They light our paths, through strength of will.

In universe, our hearts do soar,
Connected to the starry lore,
In every glint, a promise lies,
That hope remains within our eyes.

The Edge of Dreaming

At the edge of dreaming's shore,
Where waking ends and dreams explore,
A world of magic softly springs,
On whispers caught in twilight's wings.

The night's embrace, a velvet glove,
Enfolds the tales of stars above,
Through gates of sleep, our visions range,
In lands beyond, so still and strange.

There, castles built of moonbeams stand,
With silver spires and golden sand,
In dreams' embrace, our spirits free,
To dance across eternity.

Each vision, bright, a fleeting glance,
A fleeting whisper, sweet romance,
Upon this edge, both near and far,
We glimpse just who we truly are.

When dawn's light breaks, the dreams may fade,
Yet in our hearts, their mark is laid,
At dreaming's edge, our souls find flight,
And carry forth the gift of night.

Twin Flames

In heart of night, where shadows cling,
Two flames ignite, their spirits sing,
Through darkest hues, their light does weave,
A bond profound, in love they cleave.

Across the realms of time and space,
They find each other, face to face,
A dance of fire, eternal bright,
In union's glow, they share their light.

Though worlds apart, their spirits bind,
A love so fierce, its chains unwind,
In mirrored souls, a single blaze,
Through gloom and glow, they find their ways.

Two hearts in one, a single beat,
Their destinies in tandem meet,
Forever moving, side by side,
In passion's flame, their fears subside.

Through trials faced and tempests strong,
Their light endures, it burns so long,
Twin flames as one, they soar above,
In unity, they find their love.

Resonance and Dissonance

Waves of light and shadow play,
Harmony in discord's sway,
Ebb and flow in life's ballet,
Truths that night and day convey.

Silent echoes in the mind,
Melodies the heart does bind,
Chords unstrung by fate's design,
Beauty found in life's unwind.

Notes that shatter once were whole,
Fragments rattle, take a toll,
Yet within the broken soul,
Whispers of the past console.

In the clash of vibrant hues,
Chaos finds its own excuse,
Resonance where lines confuse,
Harmony within the ruse.

Balance sought in every tear,
Joy and pain both crystal clear,
Resonance and dissonance near,
In this dance, we persevere.

A Dance Apart

In a room of silent walls,
Echoes where no footstep falls,
Memories the mind recalls,
Shadowed by the past's great halls.

Twilight spins a story known,
Partners once, now dance alone,
In a rhythm, all their own,
Footprints where the light has shone.

Distance writes a tale of space,
Hearts once tethered, now give chase,
Seeking yet another trace,
Of the love that left no base.

In this ceaseless, quiet flight,
Loneliness becomes the night,
Stars that fade from memory's sight,
Longing for a lost delight.

Yet within this void, they see,
A reflection wild and free,
In the dance, a mystery,
Of the you, and I, and we.

The Canvas of Us

Brushstrokes wide on life's grand stage,
Colors blend, a living page,
Moments captured, others cage,
In a timeless, endless rage.

Pallets rich with joy and pain,
Sun and storm on windowpane,
Every loss and every gain,
Splattered on the great terrain.

Whispers of a distant hue,
Secrets held in green and blue,
How the shades of me and you,
Found their place and truth anew.

Lines that curve and twists embrace,
Finding form without a face,
In the strokes, there's no disgrace,
Only love and boundless grace.

As the paint begins to dry,
Hearts beneath the canvas lie,
In the masterpiece, we try,
To decipher earth and sky.

Against the Grain

Paths well-trodden mark the ground,
Boundaries set, yet so profound,
In the silence comes the sound,
Of footsteps that refuse the bound.

Against the grain, a choice is made,
Walking through the dim and shade,
Creating paths that will not fade,
By every step and every blade.

Voices silent from the past,
Echoes of a spell once cast,
Truths that seem too harsh and vast,
Facing winds that blow so fast.

In defiance of the norm,
Every trial becomes the storm,
Shaping lives to new perform,
Patterns shifting, hearts grown warm.

Yet within this twisting road,
Strength and confidence bestow,
Following a path bestowed,
So against the grain, we grow.

Within Reach

A hope ignites, a dream does call,
A whispered wish, though seeming small,
With every step, courage grows,
A journey starts where the wind blows.

Each day unfolds a canvas clear,
Brushstrokes of faith, they persevere,
In fields of doubt, flowers bloom,
A heart can soar beyond the gloom.

Upon the horizon, sun will rise,
Casting away the darkest ties,
An outstretched hand, a grasp so tight,
In dawn's embrace, the soul takes flight.

Beyond Grasp

Stars above, so far away,
In night's soft veil, they dance and play,
Their light a whisper, faint yet keen,
In dreams they dwell, a silver sheen.

A breath of wind, a fleeting touch,
We chase the mirage, seeking much,
Yet every step, they drift afar,
Elusive truths, like distant stars.

With open arms, we reach in vain,
For echoes lost in time's refrain,
Beyond the grasp, yet in the heart,
A yearning ache, a work of art.

Of Tides and Time

Waves crest and fall, an ocean's sigh,
In rhythm with the midnight sky,
A timeless dance, the moon's soft beam,
Reflects the past, like a wistful dream.

The sands of time, they slip away,
Each grain a moment, night or day,
In tidal pools, the echoes lie,
Of days gone by and days to try.

Seashell whispers, stories old,
In hands of time, they're gently told,
Eternal tides, relentless flow,
Through years and waves, they ebb and glow.

Chasing Light

In shadows deep, where dreams reside,
A glint of hope, our hearts confide,
We chase the light, through darkened halls,
Its grace reveals, where twilight falls.

Through misty morns and dusky eves,
A trail of stars, our sight deceives,
Yet in the chase, a truth we find,
A beacon bright, within the mind.

For every dusk, a dawn awaits,
Beyond the night, the light creates,
A path anew, with rays so pure,
In darkness deep, it finds the cure.

The Quiet Truth

In silent woods, where shadows lay,
A gentle breeze, a whispered sway,
The pines they hum, a secret sound,
In nature's arms, truths are found.

The river's song, a soothing rhyme,
It tells of peace, beyond our time,
In quiet streams, clear and still,
The heart discerns, the world's will.

Amidst the calm, where thoughts do cease,
A silent truth awards us peace,
Within the hush, the soul finds ground,
In whispered winds, true paths are found.

Woven Whispers

In twilight's tender, quiet weave,
Dreams nestle where the heart believes.
Soft murmurs through the night air cleave,
Secrets only dawn retrieves.

Through forest shadows, light will thread,
Whispers woven, silent spread.
A dance of spirits overhead,
In moonlit silks, their stories said.

The breeze, a gentle weaver's hand,
Guides whispers over sea and land.
In night's great tapestry, they stand,
Patterns only hearts withstand.

Embrace the night, where quiet speaks,
Beneath the stars, on velvet peaks.
There, woven whispers' solace seeks,
In shadows, hope's soft courage leaks.

When morning paints the dark away,
And whispers fade with break of day,
Hold tight the threads that softly sway,
They're woven in hearts, come what may.

Hidden in Plain Sight

Among the bustling crowd, unseen,
Lives a dream in silken sheen.
Masked by routine's dull, daily sheen,
In plain sight, a soul serene.

Shadowed corners, eyes divert,
Truths lie plain, yet none assert.
In open air, with silent flirt,
Hidden gems the crowds subvert.

Beneath the noise, the world conceals,
Whispers of the heart it feels.
In open hearts, the truth reveals,
A secret in the light that heals.

The mundane's cloak hides bright delight,
In routines, wonders pure and bright.
Hidden in the plainest sight,
Are stories waiting for the light.

Look deeply 'neath the surface sheer,
Past the veil of day-to-day we steer.
In the obvious, so clear,
Lie treasures hidden, ever near.

Shades of Reason

Colors dance in thought's domain,
Beyond the black and white we reign.
In shades of reason, truth's refrain,
Complex hues where wisdom's gained.

Gray hues blend where light meets dark,
In juxtaposition, insights spark.
Through reason's spectrum, minds embark,
To find the light within the dark.

Not all is clear, not all is bright,
In shadows dwell the seeds of light.
In shades of reason, black to white,
Perspective births from subtle sight.

Where reason treads, the truth unfolds,
Inquiring minds to seek and hold.
Through varied shades, beyond the bold,
In contradictions, wisdom's told.

In every hue, a lesson seeps,
Through the colors of the mind it creeps.
In shades of reason, vision leaps,
Wisdom's depth in varied keeps.

Lost in Echoes

In caverns deep, where echoes dwell,
Old stories rise, old voices swell.
Lost in echoes' mystic spell,
Time's secret tales persist and tell.

Whispers ricochet off stone,
Resounding truths not widely known.
Through endless halls, their tones are sown,
In echoes, past and present grown.

In silence, echoes seem to shout,
Reverb of fears and dreams about.
Lost in the cyclical route,
Truths that echo, felt throughout.

With every step, memories wake,
Each sound a ripple in the lake.
Ethereal journeys we undertake,
In echoes, paths of dreams we make.

Listen close, where echoes sing,
In caverns dark, where memories cling.
Lost in echoes, hopes take wing,
To future realms their calls they bring.

Milton Keynes UK
Ingram Content Group UK Ltd.
UKHW020116070624
443692UK00004B/89